Explaining
Christian
Giving

Dale Appleby

Sovereign World

ISBN: 1 85240 079 X

Scripture quotations are taken from the HOLY BIBLE, NEW INTERNATIONAL
VERSION. Copyright © 1973, 1978, 1984 by International Bible Society.
Used by permission.

This Sovereign World book is distributed in North America by Renew Books,
a ministry of Gospel Light, Ventura, California, USA. For a free catalog of resources
from Renew Books/Gospel Light, please contact your Christian supplier
or call 1-800-4-GOSPEL.

SOVEREIGN WORLD LIMITED
P.O. Box 777, Tonbridge, Kent TN11 0ZS, England.

Typeset and printed in the UK by Sussex Litho Ltd, Chichester, West Sussex.

Contents

Contents

Introduction

Giving is one of the most sensitive issues in church life. Appeals for money can stir up congregations like an intruder in an ant nest. "The church is always after money," some say. Even normally placid members can get angry when asked for money. But discussions about giving do not have to start arguments. They could start a revival. Christian giving is a blessing.

Giving is one of God's favourite subjects. It is also an exciting subject. There are riches in this subject that are much greater than money. Giving takes us to the heart of being a Christian. It also brings us up against one of the most powerful idols we face.

That is what makes giving such a difficult matter. It puts us in the middle of a big conflict. All over the world there is strong pressure to be rich: or at least to own many of the possessions that modern life can provide. It does not matter whether we are rich or poor. Both rich and poor can set their hopes on getting more money or possessions. Even in poor communities the same conflict is present. Will we set our hopes on material things to give us life, or will we trust God to supply what we need?

These questions do not stop us from working hard. They do not stop us helping the poor improve their living conditions. But they do help us work out who our God is. Trusting God for our material needs allows us to give generously. It frees us from having to keep all our money and possessions for our own needs. It helps both poor and rich share what they have.

This book gives an overview of what the Bible says about giving. We will look at the Old Testament rules for giving and outline the principles of giving that are taught there. We then study the New Testament to see what the early Christians did and why they gave as they did. Finally we will try to summarise the biblical teaching. Our aim is to work out the main principles

5

which guide Christians in their giving.

It is important to look at the biblical ideas because some people ignore them altogether while others latch on to just one idea – usually tithing. It is surprising how many of our ideas come from Christian tradition rather than from the Bible.

As you read this book I hope that you will come to a deeper understanding of God's generous ways and experience a new freedom to give as God gives.

I urge you to read the Bible references listed because they contain the main content of this book.

1

The Old Testament

The people of the Old Testament can teach us a lot about giving. They had to follow many rules. Rules which told people what kinds of things to give, and when to give them. There were many kinds of sacrifices and offerings (we will look at some of them in this section). Animals, food and money were given. But they did more than obey rules.

The people of Israel were liberal and generous givers. They were urged to give to the poor and needy. They had been refugees in a foreign land and were told to care for the strangers and foreigners in their land. The people of Israel had open hands and open hearts. We can see this at the time when the Tent of Meeting was first made, and when the Temple was built. Many people gave gifts and precious objects to the building.

This is an exciting story, so we will explore the details. Let us see what the Old Testament says about giving.

1. What Did They Give?

1.1 The Firstfruits of the Ground
The firstfruits were the first things harvested from the crop. When the people came into the land of Canaan they were to offer the firstfruits of their land. This was to to show that they were thankful for all the Lord's goodness to them (Deuteronomy 26:1-11).

The firstfruits of the oil, wine, grain and wool were to be given to the Lord for various offerings. The best of the firstfruits of their soil was to be brought to the house of the Lord (Exodus 23:19; 34:26). These firstfruits provided food for the priests (Exodus 23:19; Numbers 18:12,13; Deuteronomy 18:4). *"All the land's firstfruits that they bring to the LORD will be yours. Everyone in your household who is ceremonially clean may eat it."* (Numbers 18:13).

The Feast of Harvest was one of the three great Festivals. Once a year the people were to celebrate the Lord's goodness with the firstfruits of their crops (Exodus 23:16; 34:22).

Notice that they were told to give the best and finest of their firstfruits to the Lord (Exodus 23:19; 34:26; Numbers 18:12). This idea also occurs in teaching about other offerings. For example the fellowship offering was to be an animal without defect (Leviticus 3:1). Only the best was given to the Lord.

1.2   The First Born

The first born sons of Israel and the first born males of all the livestock were to be consecrated to the Lord. The sons were to be redeemed, as were the unclean animals (Numbers 18:15). Donkeys could also be redeemed (Exodus 13:13). The first born belonged to the Lord because he had killed the first born of Egypt and rescued the Israelites (Exodus 13:14-16). In this case also the consecrated animals were for the Levites.

1.3   Offerings

All the offerings to the Lord were to be given and what was not consumed was for the priests (Numbers 18:8-32). These included burnt offerings of animals from the flock (Leviticus 1:3); grain offerings of fine flour (Leviticus 2:1); fellowship or peace offerings of animals (Leviticus 3:1); guilt offerings (Leviticus 7:2) and others.

1.4   Gleanings

The gleanings of the field were to be left for the poor. The gleanings were the parts of the crop which were not gathered the first time. The harvesters were not to go back and reap the bits they missed. They were to leave them for the poor (Deuteronomy 24:19-22). *"When you reap the harvest of your land, do not reap to the very edges of your field or gather the gleanings of your harvest. Leave them for the poor and the alien. I am the LORD your God."* (Leviticus 23:22). An example of how this worked can be seen in the book of Ruth (Ruth 2:15-18). Boaz wanted to be kind to Ruth and told his workers to leave extra stalks for her to gather (Ruth 2:15,16).

1.5 Unused Land

Every seventh year they were not to grow anything on their land. In the seventh year, the ground was to be left for the poor. *"...during the seventh year let the land lie unplowed and unused. Then the poor among your people may get food from it, and the wild animals may eat what they leave. Do the same with your vineyard and your olive grove."* (Exodus 23:11). Leviticus 25:1-7 suggests that whatever grew of itself could be used by anyone. This may be a more general statement of the principle in Exodus 23.

1.6 Gifts and Loans

Gifts and loans were to be given to the poor (Proverbs 22:9; Deuteronomy 15:7-11). *"If there is a poor man among your brothers in any of the towns of the land that the LORD your God is giving you, do not be hardhearted or tightfisted toward your poor brother. Rather be openhanded and freely lend him whatever he needs... Give generously to him and do so without a grudging heart..."* (Deuteronomy 15:7,8,10).

1.7 Gifts for the Temple

On two occasions the people gave gifts and offerings for the sanctuary. In the time of Moses the people provided the materials to make and furnish the Tent of Meeting (Exodus 25:2-8; 35:4-9, 20-29). *"...everyone who was willing and whose heart moved him came and brought an offering to the LORD for the work on the Tent of Meeting..."* (Exodus 35:21). These gifts included gold, silver, and bronze; yarn, linen, skins, wood, olive oil, spices and precious stones.

In David's last years he gave a great amount for the building of the Temple. In response to his generosity the leaders of Israel also gave generously (1 Chronicles 29:1-19). *"The people rejoiced at the willing response of their leaders, for they had given freely and wholeheartedly to the LORD. David the king also rejoiced greatly."* (1 Chronicles 29:9). David and the leaders gave gold,

9

silver, bronze, iron, precious stones, wood and other things for the Temple.

1.8 Tithes

Tithes were also given. Abram gave a tenth of the spoils of his raid to Melchizedek (Genesis 14:20), and Jacob promised the Lord a tenth of all that the Lord gave him (Genesis 28:22). It seems this was a common practice. Other nations practised some kind of tithe, sometimes as a tax, sometimes as devotion to a god after a battle. No explanation is given as to why Abram and Jacob did so.

Later, in the time of Moses, rules for the tithe were given. The people were told to tithe the crops and the fruit from the trees, as well as the animals of the flock (Leviticus 27:30,32).

The instructions for the tithe can be summarised as follows.

a) In Leviticus 27:30-33 the tithe was for the Lord, but Numbers 18:21-24 says that the tithe was to be given to the Levites in return for their work in the Tent of Meeting. This seems to be the main idea. The tithes were used to provide for the Levites.

b) However in Deuteronomy 12:17-19; 14:22-27 the people were instructed to take their tithe each year to the sanctuary and eat it themselves in a great feast – a celebration of God's goodness. They were to include the Levites in the feast.

c) A third use of the tithe is seen in Deuteronomy 14:28-29; 26:12, where every third year the people were to lay up the tithe in their towns for the Levite, the sojourner, the fatherless and the widows.

It is not clear how we are to understand these different instructions. Some think they are different rules for different conditions and times. On this theory the tithe developed from b) to c) to a). That is, it moved from being the food of celebration to become the means of providing for the Levites. On the other hand the different passages may describe different things that were all done together: an annual feast at the sanctuary which included the

Levite, plus every third year a special gathering of the tithes for the needy. It is possible that not all the tithes were consumed at the feast. Perhaps the rest were given to the Levites.

1.9 Summary
The people of the Old Testament gave different kinds of things. Gold, silver and other precious metals; food, crops, money, animals, and the use of their land were just part of the riches given by the people of Israel.

2. To Whom Was It Given?

2.1 The Levites
Sometimes we assume that offerings were given to the Lord. The Old Testament draws a larger picture. While the offerings and tithes were given to the Lord, a large part of those offerings was handed on to the Levites. The tithes were meant to provide for the Levites who worked in the sanctuary. Even then the people used some of the tithes themselves to have a celebration in the Lord's presence.

2.2 Buildings
On two occasions offerings were given specifically for buildings and their furnishings.

2.3 The Poor
Notice the great concern for the poor in the Old Testament. Some of the tithes were to be given to the needy. The poor were also able to glean the fields and get food from the unused land. The people of Israel were encouraged to be generous to the poor.

3. How Was The Giving To Be Done?

Here is a very interesting thing. The Israelite was to give liberally, generously, freely (Proverbs 3:27,28; 11:24,25; 22:9), and with an open hand. They were not to be hardhearted or tightfisted, nor to give with a grudging heart (Deuteronomy 15:7-11). They were to give willingly as their hearts moved them (Exodus 25:2; 35:21; 1 Chronicles 29:17). Their motivation was much deeper than just keeping rules.

"If there is a poor man among your brothers in any of the towns of the land that the LORD your God is giving you, do not be hardhearted or tightfisted towards your brother. Rather be openhanded and freely lend him whatever he needs. ...Give generously to him and do so without a grudging heart; then because of this the LORD your God will bless you in all your work and in everything you put your hand to." Deuteronomy 15:7,8,10).

I encourage you to read these passages again and ask God to speak to you about the attitudes that are described.

But why did they act like this?

4. On What Basis Were The Gifts Given?

In some cases the Lord just claimed things as his own. The tithe is an example of something which the Lord regarded as his (Leviticus 27:30) because he had provided everything for the people.

God's people gave because the Lord was generous and bountiful to them. That is why they were to give things away to others (Genesis 28:20-22; Deuteronomy 26:10,11). This was especially clear when the Temple was built. The generous gifts of the people were a result of the abundant goodness of the Lord. *"But who am I, and who are my people, that we should be able to give as generously as this? Everything comes from you, and we have given you only what comes from your hand... O LORD our God, as for all this abundance that we have provided for building you a temple for your Holy Name, it comes from your hand, and all of it belongs to you."* (1 Chronicles 29:14,16). It wasn't even that they had to trust the Lord to give them back what they had given. He had already given them so much that they could share it with others. It was from his generous supply that they gave the firstfruits and offerings to him.

Nevertheless, God generously blesses our generosity (Proverbs 22:9). *"One man gives freely, yet gains even more; another withholds unduly, but comes to poverty."* (Proverbs 11:24).

Generous giving is like a circle. God gives generously to us. We give generously in response and then God continues to be generous to us. It appears that we can't give too much away when we are acting generously in response to God's abundance because he in turn gives liberally to us.

5. Later Problems in Giving

Other important references to giving in the Old Testament are in Nehemiah 10:34-39 and Malachi 3:6-12, which are applications of texts we have already looked at.

Although the law of Moses gave clear instructions about giving tithes and offerings the people of Israel did not always do what was written.

After the exile Nehemiah recorded a new commitment by the people to care for the house of God and not to neglect their offerings. The neglect of God's commands had been one of the reasons for the exile (Nehemiah 9:32-37). In a solemn assembly the leaders of the people made a written agreement to keep the laws of the Lord (Nehemiah 9:38). This included bringing the tithes, the firstfruits, the first born and wood for the temple service (Nehemiah 10:34-39).

Some time after this Malachi told the people that they were not giving what God had commanded. They were to bring the whole of their tithes and offerings. When they did, he said, the old promises would be kept. God would pour out a great blessing.

"'Bring the whole tithe into the storehouse, that there may be food in my house. Test me in this', says the LORD Almighty, 'and see if I will not throw open the floodgates of heaven and pour out so much blessing that you will not have room enough for it.'" (Malachi 3:10).

6. Summary

In the Old Testament the people of God responded to his provision by returning to him some of what he had given. Some offerings reminded them that God had rescued them from Egypt. But it was not just a matter of giving to God, these gifts were also for those who served. The food and animals they gave supported the Levites who ministered in the sanctuaries. The people also used what he had given to celebrate his goodness in feasts. In this case the people themselves ate what had been offered to God. But not all giving was directed to God and the sanctuary. The people of Israel gave generously to the poor and alien, and on two occasions they gave freely and wholeheartedly to build the sanctuaries.

The spirit of giving in the Old Testament was free, generous and wholehearted. It was not produced by law but came from generous and willing hearts. It arose from God's generous abundance to his people.

So we learn from the Old Testament that:

- God supplies an abundant bounty to his people.

- On two famous occasions the Old Testament believers gave willingly, generously and enthusiastically to building projects.

- A variety of things were given to God (and were used to provide for the Levites).

- Their methods of giving acknowledged that God provided: all was his.

- There was great concern for the poor and needy.

- The dominant descriptions of the people are that they were liberal, generous, open-hearted, open-handed, and willing.

What about your hand and heart? Although we have only surveyed the Old Testament, and still need the perspective of the cross to understand its meaning for us, there is already enough encouragement to act in a generous way. Do you have a similar attitude to the Old Testament believers? Do you have a generous heart and an open hand?

2

The New Testament

The New Testament view of giving reflects the changed economic and social conditions of the time. Judah was under Roman rule. It was part of a Roman economy. Not everyone lived and worked on the land. Many lived in cities and were involved in business and commerce. Society was more mixed. Jews lived amongst people of many races.

As the gospel spread Christians were found throughout the Roman empire. Increasingly they were Gentiles and not Jews. Churches were made up of Jews and Gentiles. They also included people from different races who used different languages (although Greek was their common language). Because the Temple was not a part of the life of most Christians many of the regulations about giving became irrelevant.

A broader question concerned whether Gentile Christians should have to keep the Old Testament law. This was a big debate in the early church. Did the old rules about giving apply to them at all?

For the first 300 years the church existed in a hostile environment. Both Jews and Romans persecuted it to different degrees. Generally the church met in homes (1 Corinthians 16:19) or hired halls (Act 19:9,10). It had no buildings of its own. Not many Christian workers were paid by the church.

There were also many poor people who were helped by other Christians (Acts 4:32-35; 6:1). Sometimes being a Christian resulted in loss of property (Hebrews 10:34) or job. There was a great famine throughout the Roman world in the time of Claudius (AD 45-47) which affected both Jews and Christians. Christians in other parts of the world sent money to help the needy people in Judea (Acts 11:28-30).

So the social, religious, and economic context of the first Christians was different to that of the Old Testament people of Israel. The instructions about giving in the New Testament reflect these changed conditions. However the general principles are the same as the Old Testament. Although the details are different, it is remarkable that the attitudes and motivations are unchanged.

Let us look at what the New Testament says about giving. This is exciting and dramatic teaching which will continue to transform our discipleship if we obey it.

7.   Tithing in the New Testament

We will start by looking at what the New Testament says about tithing. We will do this not because tithing is the most important form of giving, but because it is the one which many Christians think the Bible commands.

Although tithing was not the only form of giving in the Old Testament, it was a significant part of it. It is surprising, therefore, that there is no mention at all of the tithe or, for that matter, any of the other Old Testament offerings being required of Christians. Was this because the New Testament assumed that Christians would keep doing what the Old Testament required? No doubt the Jewish Christians in Jerusalem did keep the regulations – at least at first. Or is there more to it than that? What does the New Testament actually say about tithing? What does it teach about Gentile Christians keeping the Old Testament law?

7.1   Tithing in the New Testament
The only references to tithing in the New Testament are in the context of Old Covenant Judaism.

Jesus rebuked the teachers of the law and the Pharisees for tithing such small things as spices from their garden, while neglecting justice, mercy and faithfulness (Matthew 23:23; Luke 11:42). Jesus did not say they should practise justice instead of tithing. He said they should have done both. He made the exaggerated comparison because he thought their neglect of justice was very bad. But he still expected them to keep the law of Moses.

Jesus also told a parable about a man who was confident of his own righteousness (Luke 18:9-13). In this story of the Pharisee and the tax collector, the Pharisee referred to his tithing as evidence that he was righteous. Jesus said that the man who asked for mercy was the one who went home justified.

The writer to the Hebrews referred to Abraham offering tithes to Melchizedek (Hebrews 7:2,4-10). This is a part of his argument that Melchizedek was greater than Levi. The passage has nothing to do with the way Christians should give.

Neither Jesus, Paul, nor the writer to the Hebrews suggested that their disciples should tithe. The passages referred to above are all of the references to tithing in the New Testament. All of them are set in the context of Old Covenant Judaism. None of them is in the context of Christian giving.

7.2   Gentiles and the Law

There is certainly no reinforcement of the Old Testament methods of giving for the Gentile Church. Acts 15 is a crucial passage. At the time when Gentiles first entered the church it was made clear that they were under no obligation to keep the Old Testament law. Paul argued strongly for this general principle in a number of places (e.g. Romans 4-8, and Galatians).

To understand this we need to remember that the first Christians were Jews, or Gentiles who had attached themselves to Judaism. It was not until the Gentile Cornelius was converted (Acts 10,11), that Gentiles began to enter the church. This posed great problems for some of the Jewish Christians. Some criticised Peter for going into the home of Gentiles and eating with them (Acts 11:2,3). No doubt they would have had problems with Peter baptising the Gentiles too, if it had not been for Peter's explanation (Acts 11:4-17). They were surprised that God was including Gentiles in his people. When they heard what Peter had to say they had no further objections (Acts 11:18).

However the problem did not go away. Acts 15 records the occasion when Jewish Christians from Judea went to Antioch. They taught that *"unless you are circumcised, according to the custom taught by Moses, you cannot be saved,"* (Acts 15:1). Paul and other teachers at Antioch objected strongly. The result was a conference in Jerusalem. Paul and Barnabas, representing the church in Antioch, met with the apostles and elders in Jerusalem. Peter asked the pro-circumcision group *"...why do you try to test*

God by putting on the necks of the disciples a yoke that neither we nor our fathers have been able to bear?" (Acts 15:10). In the end the apostles and elders agreed to write to the Gentile churches and not to put on them any burden apart from some rules about how they behaved towards idol worship (Acts 15:23-30).

The effect of this decision was to free the Gentile churches from any obligation to follow the Old Testament laws. It agreed with the teaching of Paul about the place of law in the life of Christians (both Jew and Gentile) (Romans 7:1-6). The Christian life was to be lived by faith in the grace of God (Romans 5:20-6:14). While the law still described the character of the righteous person it was not to be used as a means of attaining or maintaining that righteousness. Instead believers were to live by the Spirit (Romans 8:1-8).

Paul's surprising solution to dealing with sin was not to apply the law, but grace (Romans 5:20,21). Our death with Christ has ended our obligation to the law. Our new life is lived under the rule of a new master: grace (Romans 6:14) or the Spirit (Romans 7:6).

This freedom from law together with the absence of instruction to tithe in the New Testament must force us to look in a different place for teaching about Christian giving.

7.3   Abraham's Tithe

Before we do that we need to consider an argument based on the passages in Genesis. The tithe of Abraham and the promise of tithing made by Jacob could be seen as models for everybody. But the two passages in Genesis are not the basis for a rule of tithing in either the Old or New Testament. They were both voluntary responses of an appropriate kind. They were the kind of thing other people did in those days. Tithing was a common practice.

Tithing in the law of Moses was not related to Abraham and Jacob. Its basis was God's claim to receive it. It was also given as the inheritance of the Levites.

Furthermore the Old Testament believer did much more than tithe. It is a mistake to isolate the tithe as though it was the whole of what the Old Testament expected of God's people. We have already seen that it was only a part.

7.4 Christian Practice in the First Few Centuries

It is interesting to note that many of the Christians in the period following the New Testament saw the tithe as a thing of the past. Irenaeus (130-200 AD) thought it was a Jewish law not required of Christians, who should give without external restraint. He contrasted the Old Testament obligation to tithe with the Christian's obligation to set aside all for the Lord's purpose. Origen (185-254 AD) also viewed tithes as things to be far exceeded by Christians. Chrysostom (345-405) said it was a shame that Christians only gave a tithe, when the Israelites gave tithes and additional tithes and helped widows, orphans and strangers.

However the Didache (a small book of instructions about Christian living, written about 150 AD) encouraged Christians to tithe and give their first fruits to support the teachers or the poor. Later writers such as Jerome and Augustine tended to emphasise the tithe more than the larger New Testament challenge.

7.5 Christian Tradition

Many churches have adopted tithing as one of their main traditions. Conservative and evangelical churches used to be the ones who promoted tithing. More recently churches from other traditions have also seen tithing as a useful method of giving. One of the attractions of tithing is that it gives people a clear guide-line about how much to give. There are variations of the tithe. Some have suggested a graduated tithe for those who have more money. This means that a person with a higher income can give a percentage greater than 10%.

But there are two difficulties with the promotion of tithing. One is that the Bible gives us no support for this tradition. The other is that it takes attention away from the much better biblical teaching about giving.

At this stage not everyone will agree with what I have written. So let us examine in more detail what the New Testament says about giving. Again I encourage you to look up the Bible references. The Bible contains wonderful promises which we should read and know.

8. What Did Christians Give in the New Testament?

The New Testament describes the giving of a variety of things, not just money.

8.1 Possessions
Christians shared their possessions (Acts 4:32), because they were of one heart and mind. This passage is worth thinking about. None of the believers claimed that any of their possessions was their own. Although later it became obvious that not everyone did this (Acts 5:1), it is a shocking contrast to modern ideas of personal property. Ideas of legal ownership can easily become a belief that what we have is just for ourselves. We can think that, just because we own something, we do not have to consider sharing it, or giving it away. Legal ownership does not exclude God's higher authority in our life.

Some of the first Christians sold their land or houses and gave the money to the apostles to help the needy (Acts 4:34,35). This too is a startling thing. They converted significant capital assets into cash for the sake of the poor.

These days some churches are using money or assets to buy land or buildings which can be used for the poor. Some have set up training farms. Others provide low cost loans to help people start a small business. Others use their assets in other ways to help the poor and needy, perhaps by building a dam which can help a whole community.

8.2 Food
We know that, in the early days, there was a daily distribution of food to widows and other needy people in Jerusalem (Acts 6:1). We can guess that some of the money given to the apostles was used to buy this food. But it is possible that some people gave food from their gardens or farms.

8.3 Money
Paul urged the Corinthians to put aside money from their income each week so that they could contribute to the gift being sent to Jerusalem (1 Corinthians 16:2).

"All good things" is Paul's description of what should be shared by the pupil with the teacher (Galatians 6:6). I think this means money and material things, rather than telling the teacher how much they have been blessed.

8.4 People
People were sometimes given by churches. Epaphroditus was a messenger sent to Paul by the church at Philippi to take care of his needs – even at the risk of his life (Philippians 2:25-30). This same church at Philippi sent aid to Paul on a number of occasions (Philippians 4:16).

8.5 Hospitality
Gifts that were part of hospitality feature in the life of the early church. For example, Paul urged Titus to make sure two of his friends had everything they needed for their journey (Titus 3:13).

8.6 Summary
Mostly money was given. But material goods, assets, food, and all the things that are part of hospitality were also given. Even people were given to help others.

9. To Whom Was It Given?

9.1 The Poor
The overwhelming emphasis in the New Testament is on giving to the poor and needy. This is partly due to the attention given to Paul's great collection for the poor in Jerusalem.

Jesus taught the same principle as the Old Testament: *"Give to the one who asks you, and do not turn away from the one who wants to borrow from you."* (Matthew 5:42; Luke 6:30). Giving is directed to those who have a need and ask.

Needy fellow Christians were also the object of gifts (Acts 4:34,35; Romans 12:8; Galatians 2:10; 6:7-10). *"If anyone has material possessions and sees his brother in need but has no pity on him, how can the love of God be in him?"* (1 John 3:17).

A remarkable feature of the New Testament is the great collection for the poor in Jerusalem. The initiative for this seems to have come from a prophecy by Agabus that there would be a famine throughout the Roman world. When they heard this prophecy the disciples in Antioch decided to send gifts to their fellow Christians in Judea (Acts 11:27-30). The story of how this gift was collected and taken to Jerusalem by Paul and others winds its way through the New Testament (Acts 24:17; 1 Corinthians 16:1-4; 2 Corinthians 8:4,14; 9.1; Romans 15:25-28).

This emphasis on giving to the poor is not always seen in the modern church. Most church discussions about money are related to paying the church's bills.

9.2   The Workers

A second emphasis is on giving to the labourer. The *"worker is worth his keep"* according to Jesus (Matthew 10:10).

Paul, the apostle, valued the support of the Philippians in his apostolic mission into Macedonia (Philippians 4:14-20). Although at Corinth and elsewhere Paul supported himself, in this case he was helped by the Philippian church. He believed that the apostles were entitled to be supported in their work, even though he did not make use of this right himself (1 Corinthians 9:1-18).

Paul's argument extends to the evangelist. *"...the Lord has commanded that those who preach the gospel should receive their living from the gospel."* (1 Corinthians 9:14).

The elders who direct the affairs of the church are worthy of double honour, according to Paul (1 Timothy 5:17,18). 'Honour' probably refers to some kind of pay (see GNB, NEB). Double may mean double what is paid to widows, or it may be a general idea such as 'ample provision'. Paul especially identifies those whose work is preaching and teaching. This may be because of the importance Paul attaches to these ministries, and also because of the time required to do that work. Notice that the same Old Testament text is used in 1 Corinthians 9:9, *"Do not muzzle the ox while it is treading out the grain."* (Deuteronomy 25:4). Paul also quotes Jesus' words, *"the worker deserves his wages."* (Luke 10:7). This principle was already firmly established in the Old Testament (Leviticus 19:13; Deuteronomy 24:14,15).

The teacher is singled out again in Galatians (Galatians 6:6). Many take this to mean reporting the spiritual blessings received, but I do not think Paul would have spiritualised it so easily. He is referring to sharing material blessings.

These passages show different expressions of the principle that certain Christian workers ought to be provided for. This matter of giving to the labourer may require more study by the modern church. Some churches have drifted into practices through historical circumstances rather than establishing their practice on biblical principles. There seems to be an assumption among some churches and missionary groups that Christian workers ought to live in simple poverty, or only have their basic needs provided for. The principles referred to above seem to be different to that.

9.3 Giving So Others Can Hear the Gospel

Jesus began the parable of the shrewd manager by referring to *"a rich man whose manager was accused of wasting his possessions."* (Luke 16:1). Jesus concluded the story by saying, *"I tell you, use worldly wealth to gain friends for yourselves, so that when it is gone, you will be welcomed into eternal dwellings."* (Luke 16:9).

The parable tells the story of a man who was going to lose his job. He wanted to have people who would help him when he had no job, so he changed the amounts that the debtors owed his master. He hoped they would pay him back with help later.

Jesus applied the story to the way his disciples used money. He suggested that what happened later, that is after death, was more important than the benefits we get from money now. He thought we should use money now to win friends in heaven. He wanted us to use money so that people would welcome us into heaven. He did not mean that somehow money could buy our way into heaven. Rather money could be used so that people heard the gospel and ended up in heaven themselves. These people would then welcome us and thank us for using our money so that they heard the gospel.

Jesus said worldly wealth was a small thing to be trusted with (Luke 16:10-12). His teaching in this passage helps us to see money in a biblical perspective. One of its uses is to give it so others can hear the gospel.

9.4 Summary

We have asked the question, "To whom were the gifts given?" It is surprising that there is no emphasis on giving goods or money to the Lord. Giving in the New Testament is always directed to other people. Perhaps this is because Christians have already given themselves to the Lord (Romans 12:2).

Gifts were to be given to the needy, to Christian workers, and so that others could hear the gospel. There is obviously a lot of scope for applying these principles.

10. How Was It Given?

This is a very important question. Did Christians give because of rules and duty? Did they give because they were forced or persuaded into it? What motivated them?

At the beginning the giving was spontaneous. People gave according to the need (Acts 2:45). It was not regulated. It resulted from love and gratitude, and a desire to help. No doubt Christians have continued to give from these motives.

The great exposition of Christian giving is in 2 Corinthians 8 and 9. In these two chapters Paul urged the Corinthians to get their money ready for the messengers who were coming to take it to Jerusalem. This was part of Paul's great collection for the poor Christians in Judea (see Section 9.1 above). The passage states some of the basic principles of giving and contains some of the greatest encouragements to generosity in the New Testament.

10.1 Wanting to Give

Paul used the example of the Macedonians to encourage the Corinthians. At the beginning we read that the Macedonian's joy and poverty *"welled up in rich generosity"* (8:2). Paul saw this as a result of the grace of God given to the Macedonian churches (8:1). God's grace worked in them so that they took the initiative themselves. They asked to share in the gift (8:3,4). Their generosity overflowed so that they not only gave as they were able (a basic principle of giving: 8:12) but even beyond their ability (8:3). (Compare the story of the poor widow in Mark 12:43,44).

Their generous giving and compassion for the poor Christians in Judea was a result of the commitment of their lives. Paul seems to have been surprised by their actions. A contribution to the collection was what he was looking for. But *"they gave themselves first to the Lord and then to us in keeping with God's will."* (2 Corinthians 8:5). Their giving was an expression, a sign, of the wholehearted commitment they had made to the Lord. But it was more than this. It was also a commitment to Paul and his project. They recognised that what Paul was doing was God's will. They wanted to be part of the group who had contributed to this collection. A collection which had become a major commitment of Paul. It was his way of obeying the will of God which he and others had heard in Antioch – and the Macedonians wanted to be part of it.

Such enthusiasm and spiritual discernment made Paul glad, and he used the Macedonian's example to encourage the Corinthians. This is a good example of joyful giving. It is the opposite of reluctant giving.

10.2 Giving by Grace

Paul knew that everything the Corinthians had was from God (1 Corinthians 4:7). They were proud that they excelled in faith, speech, and knowledge, but Paul wanted them to excel in giving as well (2 Corinthians 8:7). Their giving was an act of grace (8:6). He urged them to excel in *"this grace of giving"* (8:7). Giving is a grace, or we could say, a charismatic gift. Giving results from the grace of God at work in our lives.

This is a very important matter. Often when churches try to raise more money they try to get it by rules, or by making people feel guilty. God's free grace is what allows Christian giving to flourish. Jesus' poverty is the great example of grace (8:9). If Jesus can give his life for us, he can certainly supply all our other needs, and we in turn can copy his example in giving to others.

Willing giving is important (8:11-12; 9:1-5). Paul commended their initiative (8:10), their willingness (8:12), their eagerness, their readiness, and their enthusiasm (9:2). All this was a result of God's grace at work in their lives.

There are other signs in this passage that giving is by grace. People should give on the basis of what they have, not on the basis of what they do not have (8:12; Acts 11:29). What they do have comes from the Lord (9:8). But it also comes from others. That is what giving is about. The Corinthians have plenty today so they share with the Christians in Judea. Another day the Christians in Judea will have plenty and can share their resources with the Corinthians when they are in need (8:14). This equality depends on God's gracious provision. It is like the manna – everyone had enough, no matter how much they gathered (8:15).

10.3 Generosity
We are to give cheerfully and decisively, not reluctantly or under compulsion (9:7); generously and not grudgingly (9:5). This giving allows us to have all that we need for our own affairs, but enough left over to do good to others as well (9:8). Our great generosity is a result of God's abounding grace to us. He gives us plenty to give away (9:10,11).

The idea that dominates this passage is generosity. Paul refers to *"rich generosity"* (8:2); *"a generous gift"* (9:5); sowing and reaping generously (9:6); being generous on every occasion (9:11); and *"your generosity"* (9:11,13).

10.4 Contentment
Such generosity assumes a freedom from the love of money. What Paul calls *"godliness with contentment"* (1 Timothy 6:6-19). This is a big problem for Christians, and undermines generous giving. Contentment means being content with food and clothing, rather than trying to get rich. It means being satisfied if we have enough for our basic needs. The desire for money causes all kinds of evils, according to Paul. Notice that it is not money which is the problem, but the love of money.

In other places Paul warns about *"greed which is idolatry"* (Colossians 3:5; Ephesians 5:3). Many societies think greed is good. People are encouraged to want more, to try to get rich, to get more and more possessions. These desires are the opposite of Christian thinking. Greed and covetousness are forms of idolatry. We can make an idol out of money or possessions. Jesus said we were not to serve *"Mammon"* (Matthew 6:24). We are not to run after even the basic necessities of life like the pagans do. Rather we are to seek God's kingdom first and trust God to supply everything that we need (Matthew 6:31-34).

Those who depend on money to supply all their needs serve the idol. They think the idol will help them, but really they are slaves to the idol. Slaves to money cannot be open handed and generous. Paul said, *"Some people, eager for money, have wandered from the faith and pierced themselves with many griefs."* (1 Timothy 6:10).

10.5 Being Rich

So is it wrong to be rich? It is not wrong, but it may be difficult (Matthew 19:23). It was difficult for the rich young man. Jesus asked him to choose between his possessions and following Jesus. He would not give up his possessions and went away sad.

Why did Jesus ask him to sell his possessions? Why were the disciples astonished? What Jesus said went against the popular ideas of his day. Many thought that the rich were the most likely to be saved because their wealth was a sign of God's blessing and approval.

Perhaps also because they had the wealth to do good, people thought they were more likely to be saved. They were free from always working just to provide food for themselves and so could do good to others, and contribute to the religious life of the people. Some people might have thought these good deeds gave them an advantage in gaining God's approval. The rich young man asked Jesus what good thing he needed to do to get eternal life. He wanted to do things with his time and money that would provide him with the life eternal.

In contrast to this, Jesus offered eternal life if he followed him. Although the man's wealth seemed to be an advantage, it had become an idol. Jesus asked him to sell his possessions so that he could obey Jesus. In this case the man's possessions were a danger because they tempted the man to rely on them rather than on Jesus. The great danger was that once he relied on them he would devote his life to them, although they were not able to give him eternal life.

Nevertheless, even though it is difficult to be a Christian and to be wealthy, it is not in itself wrong. Wealth is a blessing from God, and has to be used in the way that he wants. Paul urged Timothy to encourage the rich in two ways (1 Timothy 6:17-19).

One had to do with their trust. They were not to be arrogant or to put their hope in wealth. Rather they were to put their hope in God. Riches are uncertain. God is reliable and *"richly provides us with everything for our enjoyment."* Here is one of the difficulties for the rich: to see God as the provider of their wealth, and to trust him, rather than to centre their life on their riches.

Secondly, Timothy was to command the rich to do good and to be generous. They were to be rich in good deeds. Generosity and a willingness to share were to mark their lives. These were traditional expectations of the wealthy. Public benefactors were highly regarded then, as they are now. But in this case their reward is not in the present age. They do not give in order to win the approval of their fellow citizens. That is why giving is to be done without show (Matthew 6:2-4). Instead, by generously giving their riches away, they are storing up treasure for the age to come. They give in secret knowing that their Father in heaven sees what they are doing. They do not gain eternal life by this means, but they do act in a way that shows where their true life comes from. Their priority is to store up treasure in heaven. Like Abraham they are citizens of another country and are banking their assets in the bank of that heavenly country (Hebrews 11:9,10). They know that their Father who sees what is done in secret will reward them (Matthew 6:4).

"Command those who are rich in this present world not to be arrogant nor to put their hope in wealth, which is so uncertain, but to put their hope in God, who richly provides us with everything for our enjoyment. Command them to do good, to be rich in good deeds, and to be generous and willing to share. In this way they will lay up treasure for themselves as a firm foundation for the coming age, so that they may take hold of the life that is truly life." (1 Timothy 6:17-19).

10.6 Summary

So what does the New Testament say about how to give? The general idea is the same as the Old Testament – with open hearted generosity. This generosity results from God's gracious gifts to us. It is also a result of knowing the future: it is a way of storing up treasure in heaven.

11.   What Was The Basis of Giving?

11.1   God is Generous

The basis is the same as the Old Testament – the gracious and generous gifts of God (Matthew 10:8). We trust God to supply our needs (Matthew 6:25-34; Philippians 4:19). We know he will supply what we need and also give us enough to give to those in need. Indeed we know that he has already given us enough to share.

"And God is able to make all grace abound to you, so that in all things at all times, having all that you need, you will abound in every good work. As it is written: 'He has scattered abroad his gifts to the poor; his righteousness endures forever.' Now he who supplies seed to the sower and bread for food will also supply and increase your store of seed and will enlarge the harvest of your righteousness. You will be made rich in every way so that you can be generous on every occasion, and through us your generosity will result in thanksgiving to God." (2 Corinthians 9:8-11).

This is an important principle. God graciously gives us all we need. This is not just for our own needs, but also enough *"to abound in every good work."* It is enough to allow us to be *"generous on every occasion."* In other words, God is able to provide us generously with enough for ourselves and sufficient left over to give to those in need.

God's great generosity is seen both in providing us in advance with enough to give and also in giving back to us what we have given.

"Give, and it will be given to you. A good measure, pressed down, shaken together and running over, will be poured into your lap. For with the measure you use, it will be measured to you." (Luke 6:38).

11.2   Trust God

Giving means trusting God. Paul's idea, that God will supply both our needs and enough to give to the poor, does not mean we will always have extra money in the bank after we have given. Jesus taught that God supplied our needs on the basis of how we treated others. He does give to us generously from the riches of his grace.

But he also responds to our generosity. If we give in a mean way, how can we expect God to be generous to us? There is a challenge to faith in this passage. Can we use a measuring container that is too big for God to fill? Jesus stated the principle: *"For with the measure you use, it will be measured to you."* (Luke 6:38). It is a similar idea to the earlier statement, *"Do to others as you would have them do to you."* (Luke 6:31). In this case it is a matter of doing to others what we want God to do to us. Our generosity to others is a way of telling God how generous we want him to be to us. It is also a way of saying how much we trust him to be generous.

It is not possible to give more than God can supply. Some Christians need a safety net, a buffer of money or possessions that keep them safe from what they think is having too little. They have a limit to how much they will give. They want to keep some in reserve "just in case". This buffer is not the same as having plenty as a result of God's blessing. Nor is it the same as putting money aside for legitimate needs. Rather it is a form of unbelief. It is putting our trust in uncertain riches (1 Timothy 6:17). It is a form of anxiety about not having enough, and not being sure that God will look after us. Paul said he knew what it was like to be in need, and yet he had learnt to be content because he could do everything through the strength of Christ (Philippians 4:11-13). Our fear of being in need is a problem if we trust in wealth for our life. If we trust in God, it does not need to be a cause of fear. So our generosity depends on not trusting in our wealth.

A great deal of the difficulty associated with giving is a result of our anxiety about money (see Matthew 6:19-34). In three churches I have belonged to we have had appeals for large amounts of money for building projects. In each case we asked people to give directly, rather than use the common methods of fund-raising. In each of these churches we saw some people begin with a great anxiety about what would happen to them if they gave any significant amount of money. By God's grace their trust in God grew as they gradually learnt that they could not give away too much. The more they gave, the more he gave them. In some cases people received large amounts of unexpected money within days of giving generously to the project.

Unfortunately there is a popular error associated with this nowadays. It suggests that God really wants us to be rich and prosperous and the way to become rich is to give, so that the Lord will give more back to us. But the scriptures are not putting forward a magical method of getting rich. Neither do they encourage greed and covetousness. It is a great pity that many Christians have begun to centre their lives on getting rich rather than on generously giving to the poor.

11.3   God First

By contrast the Macedonians *"first gave themselves to the Lord"* (2 Corinthians 8:5). Jesus urged the same thing in the Sermon on the Mount. He warned against a preoccupation with our needs, and anxiety about our money. Instead he wanted his disciples to be concerned above all else with his kingdom and righteousness (Matthew 6:25-34). Giving flows naturally from such a lifestyle. When the cares of the world do not consume us, we can be careful for the kingdom.

11.4   Fellowship

God is the great giver and he gives to us both for our needs and for sharing with others. The needs of others will often be met from the gifts God has given to me. If my brother remains in need, it will be because I have closed my heart to him (1 John 3:17), not because God has.

All of this assumes a context of fellowship. It is clear in the New Testament (as it is in the Old Testament) that it is the family of God's people, the sharing in Christ, that is the context for this kind of giving. The Macedonians begged to be allowed to share in meeting the needs of Jewish Christians in Jerusalem. The Jerusalem Christians in turn will long for the Corinthians and pray for them because of their generosity (2 Corinthians 9:12-15). At another time when the Corinthians are in need, others will meet their need (2 Corinthians 8:13-15). It is this mutual sharing and love which is the context for Christian giving.

Therefore we not only trust God to supply, but we trust others to share. We need to be willing to receive. While it is more blessed to give than to receive (Acts 20:35), it is difficult for some

31

of us to receive from others. This is because we want to be self-sufficient and self-reliant. We do not want to be dependent. This is a form of pride and shows a lack of dependence on God. Often our needs are supplied by the generosity of others. Indeed something as simple as having a job depends on other people who provide the job, or who buy our produce.

The basis of generous giving is God's generous grace to us, and the mutual fellowship in which that grace comes to us.

3

Christian Giving

12. Principles of Christian Giving

Now that we have looked at what the Bible says about giving, we will try to put the ideas together. What can we say about the way Christians should give? What are the main principles that should shape our practice?

12.1 The Old Testament showed us four main principles.

First. God was the one who supplied everything. The offerings and tithes were ways of thanking God, and acknowledging his provision. They were what he claimed because he had given them everything.

Second. The workers in the sanctuary (and the building itself) were to be provided for by the gifts of the people.

Third. The poor and needy were to be cared for.

Fourth. All this was to be done with a thankful heart, an open hand, and great generosity.

12.2 The New Testament showed us a similar picture.

First. Giving was directed to the poor, to the Christian workers and to the spread of the gospel. It is never talked about as being given to God. Christians are given to God. Their money is given to others.

Second. None of this giving was regulated. Giving appears to be much more spontaneous and motivated by a desire to help.

Third. Giving is an act of generosity. It is motivated by God's generosity to us in Christ. If the Old Testament saw God as the provider of everything, the New Testament sees Christ as the one who became poor so that we might become rich (2 Corinthians 8:9).

Fourth. It arises from a desire to participate in the work of the gospel.

As we think back on the teaching in both the Old and New Testaments, the thing that stands out is generosity. Whatever the details of what is given, or to whom it is given, the underlying motive is a generous heart. Christians should be generous givers. There is no doubt about that in the New Testament. Such liberality goes to the heart of why they are Christians.

12.3   So let us try to summarise a Christian approach to giving.

1. Christians are committed to generosity, because God is always generous to us. We believe God will always supply us with enough for ourselves and enough to give away. We believe Proverbs 11:24, and Luke 6:38.

2. We want to be like our Father, and give to the poor and needy: both Christian and non-Christian, individual and church.

3. We want to share with those who are bringing the gospel to places where the church is new or non-existent.

4. We are committed to give to the ministry of the gospel associated with our own church. That is how we share with, and provide for those who labour alongside us in the gospel. It also enables the local church to share in the work of the gospel in other places in a similar way in which the Philippians helped Paul.

12.4   Wesley's Answer
But how do we do this? Is there a way of working out how much of our income and possessions should be given to these needs?

John Wesley had a remarkable answer. His method goes to the heart of the New Testament: set your standard of living and give away the rest.

He frequently spoke about wealth and giving. One of his famous sermons was on Matthew 6:19-23 (*'Lay not up for yourselves treasures on earth...'*).

Wesley said we were not forbidden

1. to provide for what we should give to others (eg taxes);

2. to provide for our normal needs: "a sufficiency of plain wholesome food to eat, and clean raiment to put on";

3. to provide for our children and household;

4. to lay up what is needed to carry on our worldly business.

But once a person has all this, and "seeks a still larger portion on earth; he lives in open, habitual denial of the Lord that bought him. 'He has' practically 'denied the faith, and is worse than' ... an 'infidel.'" (The Works of John Wesley 3rd Edition Volume V p.368).

In his sermon on the Good Steward in Luke 16:2 Wesley put a question to his hearers. "In what manner did you employ that compulsive talent, money? not in gratifying the desires of the flesh, the desire of the eye, or the pride of life? not squandering it away in vain expenses, ...but first supplying your own reasonable wants, together with those of your family; then restoring the remainder to me, through the poor, whom I had appointed to receive it; looking upon yourself as only one of that number of poor, whose wants were to be supplied out of that part of my substance which I had placed in your hands for this purpose; leaving you the right of being supplied first, and the blessedness of giving rather than receiving? Were you accordingly a general benefactor to mankind? feeding the hungry, clothing the naked, comforting the sick, assisting the stranger, relieving the afflicted, according to their various necessities?" (The Works of John Wesley 3rd Edition Volume VI p.146).

Wesley's motto was: Gain all you can. Save all you can. Give all you can.

Just before he died, he stopped keeping his account book with the words, "For upwards of 86 years I have kept my accounts exactly, I will not attempt it any longer, being satisfied with the continuing conviction that I save all I can, and give all I can – that is all I have." (Quoted in J Wesley Bready, England: Before and after Wesley, London, Hodder and Stoughton, 1938, p.238).

In 1734 he wrote "If I leave behind me £10 ... you and all mankind bear witness against me that I lived and died a thief and robber." (Bready p238).

Wesley lived what he preached. Sales of his books often earned him large amounts. But he never spent more than £30 in a year on his personal needs. The rest he gave away. One year he gave away £1400. He always wore inexpensive clothes and dined on simple food.

12.5   How to Give

I believe that Wesley was right. Our major task is to set a limit to our affluence by deciding on a standard of living that is appropriate to the gospel and the world we live in. The problem is not how much of our income should be given away, but rather how much we should keep. Where should we set the limit to our expenditure? The Lord gives us enough for our needs and more to give away. We should decide what our needs are (rather than our wants) and give the rest away.

This may appear as though the workers and the poor are getting the left-overs. What they should be getting is the overflow of the abundance of what the Lord gives to us. In fact the labourer and the poor are often getting less than that, because we are pocketing the gifts God gave us for them, instead of sharing those gifts.

Can we trust God to supply our needs? Can we trust him when we give to those in need? There is no doubt that we can. But we should also ask, "Can God trust us to share the good things he has given us?" Are we faithful stewards of his rich bounty? Have we been spending more on ourselves than we really need? Has our heart been closed to the poor and needy? Have we shared our good things as the Lord has commanded us?

God graciously and generously gives us all things, and that is how he wants us to give to others. There are no rules. Only God's grace. It is a generous heart and an open hand that knows how to give. Such generosity towards the poor and enthusiasm for the gospel will sometimes lead us to give more than we are able. But we will give, not to show others how good we are, nor because someone has made us feel guilty, but because we have a passion for God's kingdom. Because God has changed us.

4

Take Action

When we read the Bible we should act on what we read. It is not enough to gain more information. What does God want us to do in response to what we read? This section suggests some possible responses we could make to the Bible's teaching about giving.

1. Repent

Confess to God and repent of attitudes that are different to what he wants.

Confess and repent of patterns of giving that are contrary to his Word.

2. Acknowledge

Acknowledge God's great generosity to you. Count your blessings. Give thanks.

3. Ask

Ask for a different attitude if you need to.

Ask God to continue to supply all your needs.

4. Act

Do you need to restore other people's goods? Give something that you promised? Give generously to particular people or groups? Change what you spend on yourself?

Decide what to do and then do it.

5

For Thought and Talk

This section contains some questions which could be used in small group discussions. Some could be used by church management committees. Some are suitable for personal reflection.

1. Do you think Exodus 35 and 1 Chronicles 29, provide any justification for Christians to spend money on fine church buildings? What about fine houses?

2. In what way could the widow, who only had two copper coins (Matthew 12:42), think that God had blessed her abundantly? Is it God's will for us to be materially prosperous?

3. How would you help a Christian who wanted to have a generous and giving heart?

4. Do you think that pastors should be paid according to the same standards as, for example, school teachers or nurses? Why?

5. Do you think it is better to send money to local churches in the Third World so that they can employ and support their own workers, or to pay the workers (or their missionary organisation) to go and work in those churches? Why? What biblical principles apply to this question?

6. What are the arguments for and against a Christian giving 6% of their income to the church? If you think there is a better way, what is it?

7. What do Christians need to do to bring their giving into line with the teaching of the Bible? What stops them doing this?

8. What can Christians and their churches do to give more effectively to the poor? Where are the really poor people in your country? Or in your district? How can your church help them?

9. Is it realistic to expect Christians to limit their expenditure to their real needs, and give away the rest? What would need to happen for this to take place?

10. When should possessions and property be given away rather than just income?

❖ ❖ ❖ ❖

If you have enjoyed this book and would like to help us to send a copy of it and many other titles to needy pastors in the **Third World**, please write for further information or send your gift to:

Sovereign World Trust, P.O. Box 777, Tonbridge, Kent TN11 0ZS, United Kingdom

or to the **'Sovereign World'** distributor in your country.